TITANIC

Hardcover edition first published
in the United States in 2012 by
Capstone
151 Good Counsel Dr.
Mankato, MN 56001

Conceived and produced by
Weldon Owen Pty Ltd
59-61 Victoria Street, McMahons Point
Sydney, NSW 2060, Australia

WELDON OWEN PTY LTD
Managing Director Kay Scarlett
Publisher Corinne Roberts
Creative Director Sue Burk
Production Director Todd Rechner
Images Manager Trucie Henderson

Project Editor Pip Morgan
Designer Phil Gamble
Design Assistant Emily Spencer
Picture Researcher Louise Thomas

Library of Congress Cataloging-in-Publication Data
Cataloging-in-publication information is on file with
the Library of Congress

ISBN 978-1-4296-7527-7

Printed by Hung Hing Printing Group Limited
Manufactured in China

The paper used in the manufacture of this book
is sourced from wood grown in sustainable forests.
It complies with the Environmental Management
System Standard ISO 14001:2004

A WELDON OWEN PRODUCTION

ABOUT THE AUTHOR

Philip Wilkinson has written more than 60 books, mainly
in the fields of history, architecture, and the arts. His titles
include the award-winning *Amazing Buildings*, *A Celebration
of the Customs and Rituals of the World*, which was endorsed
by the United Nations, and the bestselling *What the Romans
Did For Us*, the book of the BBC TV series of the same name.
He lives in England and the Czech Republic, and enjoys
exploring the old buildings and historical sites of these
countries, and giving talks about them.

TITANIC

Disaster at Sea

CONTENTS

THE BLUE RIBAND CUP

AN AWARD CALLED the Blue Riband was given for the fastest trip across the Atlantic Ocean. But there was no actual trophy until the Hales Cup was made in 1935. Winning the Blue Riband brought fame and honor to the major shipping lines. Cunard, with its speedy liners, was especially successful.

The Hales Cup
with Blue Riband
of 1935

SS GREAT EASTERN

Isambard Brunel designed the SS *Great Eastern* so that she could travel around the world without refueling. She had sails, steam-driven paddle wheels, and propellers.

BUILDER: J. SCOTT RUSSELL & CO.

OWNER: EASTERN COMPANY

LAUNCHED: JANUARY 31, 1858

LENGTH: 692 FT (211 M)   **BEAM:** 82 FT (25 M)

SPEED: 14 KNOTS (16 MPH / 26 KM/H)

CAPACITY: 4,418 (4,000 PASSENGERS / 418 CREW)

RMS LUCANIA

RMS *Lucania* had the largest engines of any liner of the time and won the Blue Riband in 1893. In 1901 she was the first Cunard liner to have a Marconi wireless system.

BUILDER: FAIRFIELD SHIPBUILDING

OWNER: CUNARD LINE

LAUNCHED: FEBRUARY 2, 1893

LENGTH: 622 FT (190 M)   **BEAM:** 65.25 FT (21.5 M)

SPEED: 23.5 KNOTS (27 MPH / 43.3 KM/H)

CAPACITY: 2,424 (2,000 PASSENGERS / 424 CREW)

THE GOLDEN AGE OF OCEAN LINERS

THE GREAT OCEAN LINERS were fitted with the latest, most powerful engines. Wealthy passengers stayed in luxurious cabins and staterooms, while the ships were staffed by a small army of crew. Before the invention of the airliner, these ships provided the easiest way for people to travel long distances, and were popular with both the super-rich and with poor emigrants traveling from Europe to the United States. Several shipping lines ran these huge vessels, but the most famous were the British companies Cunard and White Star.

Cunard Line
luggage tab from
RMS *Mauretania*

RMS OCEANIC

RMS *Oceanic* was the world's largest ship until 1901. During World War I she became an armed naval ship but she ran aground off Shetland, north of Scotland, in 1914.

BUILDER: HARLAND AND WOLFF

OWNER: WHITE STAR LINE

LAUNCHED: JANUARY 14, 1899

LENGTH: 704 FT (215 M)   **BEAM:** 63.8 FT (19.4 M)

SPEED: 21 KNOTS (24.2 MPH / 40 KM/H)

CAPACITY: 2,059 (1,710 PASSENGERS / 349 CREW)

BUILDING TITANIC

CONSTRUCTING ENORMOUS SHIPS such as *Titanic* and her sister vessel *Olympic* was a huge job. They were built side by side at a shipyard in Belfast, Northern Ireland, which belonged to a company called Harland and Wolff. The shipyard had to be specially adapted, and construction of the ships took two years, with up to 3,000 workers employed on each ship at any one time. The total cost of *Titanic* was £1.5 million, the equivalent of around $125 million today.

AT WORK IN THE SHIPYARD

First, the workers constructed the keel along the base of the ship. Then they built up a steel framework like a skeleton and covered it with steel plates to form the cavernous hull. Later, they added internal walls, decks, and the fixtures and fittings—from the huge funnels and engines to the luxurious decorations.

TITANIC *Tales*
THOMAS ANDREWS

Thomas Andrews was the managing director and head of the design department of Harland and Wolff. He was in charge of drawing up the detailed plans for *Titanic*. He checked every aspect of the design carefully and was responsible for making sure the ship met the owner's expectations.

WHITE STAR
ROYAL MAIL STEAMER
"TITANIC"

TITANIC *Tales*
JOSEPH BRUCE ISMAY

Bruce Ismay was the head of the White Star Line, the shipping company that owned *Titanic*. He wanted the ship to be better than the ships, such as *Mauretania*, belonging to the rival Cunard Line. He also wanted *Titanic* to be the largest and most impressive ship ever built.

QUEEN OF THE OCEAN

TITANIC WAS NOT ONLY the biggest ship on the seas, she was also the most luxurious. Inside this queen of the ocean, the White Star Line offered the highest standards of accommodation, food, and service. For those who paid the most, there was also an amazing range of facilities—from squash courts and a gymnasium to top-class restaurants and cafés—and *Titanic* and *Olympic* were the first ships to be equipped with a swimming pool and a Turkish bath.

INSIDE THE SHIP OF DREAMS

The ship's huge size meant that there was plenty of space on board. Two grand sweeping staircases linked the first-class facilities with the decks outside, and many of the public areas, such as the dining rooms, reception rooms, and smoking rooms for first- and second-class passengers, were vast. Even with more than 2,000 people on board—*Titanic* could have taken 3,547 people if it had been completely full—the ship never felt crowded.

THE WHITE STAR LINE

Titanic was owned by the White Star Line, which was a very successful shipping company. It also owned *Olympic*, which was like *Titanic* in almost every detail, and *Britannic*, which was even bigger than *Titanic*. These three ships had accommodations for both rich and poor passengers.

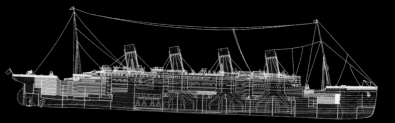

Titanic's class structure
Like most liners of the time, *Titanic* offered accommodations at three levels of comfort, or "classes." Specific areas and facilities were set aside for the different classes of passengers.

- ■ First-class areas
- ■ Second-class areas
- ■ Third-class areas
- Crew quarters

WHITE STAR TRIPLE-SCREW STEAMERS
"OLYMPIC," 45,000 TONS. AND
"TITANIC," 45,000 TONS.
THE LARGEST STEAMERS IN THE WORLD.

Selling the dream
Illustrated booklets showed the kind of accommodations in *Olympic* and *Titanic*.

Titanic's sister ship, *Olympic*, spent 24 years in service, gaining the nickname "Old Reliable."

Poop deck

WHITE STAR LINE
TRIPLE SCREW STEAMER
882½ FT. LONG   **"OLYMPIC"**   46,359 TONS

Britannic was launched in 1914 and served as a hospital ship during World War I before being sunk.

Cross section of Titanic
The ship was arranged in several floors, or decks. Engines and storage were at the lowest levels, open-air decks at the top, and cabins and public rooms between.

Funnel

Rigging

Sun deck

Lifeboats stowed here

Upper promenade deck A

Upper deck C

Promenade deck B

Saloon deck D

Main deck E

Swimming pool

Middle deck F

Squash court

Lower deck G

Orlop deck, with engines and boilers

Bilge

Stern bridge used for docking

Third-class general room

Third-class cabins

Aft well deck

Second-class cabins

Second-class dining room

SS KAISER WILHELM DER GROSSE

SS *Kaiser Wilhelm der Grosse* became the first German vessel to win the Blue Riband and the first liner, when she was working as a merchant cruiser, to be sunk in World War I.

BUILDER: STETTINER VULCAN

OWNER: NORDDEUTSCHER LLOYD

LAUNCHED: MAY 4, 1897

LENGTH: 655 FT (200.1 M)   **BEAM:** 65.8 FT (20.1 M)

SPEED: 22.5 KNOTS (25.9 MPH / 41.7 KM/H)

CAPACITY: 1,994 (1,506 PASSENGERS / 488 CREW)

RMS CARONIA

Before and after World War I, when she became a troopship, RMS *Caronia* served several destinations in Europe and America. She was sold for scrap in 1932.

BUILDER: JOHN BROWN & COMPANY

OWNER: CUNARD LINE

LAUNCHED: JULY 13, 1904

LENGTH: 678 FT (207 M)   **BEAM:** 72 FT (22 M)

SPEED: 18 KNOTS (21 MPH / 33 KM/H)

CAPACITY: 1,550 PASSENGERS

RMS LUSITANIA

RMS *Lusitania* was fast and luxurious, but smaller than the later White Star liners. She was sunk by a German U-boat during World War I, with the loss of 1,198 lives.

BUILDER: JOHN BROWN & COMPANY

OWNER: CUNARD LINE

LAUNCHED: JUNE 7, 1906

LENGTH: 787 FT (240 M)   **BEAM:** 87 FT (26.5 M)

SPEED: 26.7 KNOTS (30.7 MPH / 49.4 KM/H)

CAPACITY: 3,048 (2,198 PASSENGERS / 850 CREW)

RMS MAURETANIA

Slightly larger than her sister ship, RMS *Lusitania*, the liner RMS *Mauretania* broke the transatlantic speed record in 1907 and held the Blue Riband for 22 years.

BUILDER: SWAN, HUNTER & WIGHAM RICHARDSON

OWNER: CUNARD LINE

LAUNCHED: SEPTEMBER 20, 1906

LENGTH: 790 FT (240.8 M)   **BEAM:** 88 FT (26.8 M)

SPEED: 28.7 KNOTS (33 MPH / 53 KM/H)

CAPACITY: 2,967 (2,165 PASSENGERS / 802 CREW)

The world's largest gantry supported a crane for moving heavy materials.

Sister ships

Titanic and *Olympic* were built next to each other at the Harland and Wolff shipyard. Here, workers are covering the vessels' metal skeletons with an outer skin of steel plates.

SHIPBUILDERS

HARLAND AND WOLFF started at a small shipyard on Queen's Island, Belfast, and grew into the biggest shipbuilder in the world. The company's early success was due to the engineering skill of Edward J. Harland. His ships had metal decks to make them stronger, and hulls with flatter bottoms so they could carry more cargo. After Harland died in 1895, William James Pirrie took over and led the company to still greater successes with the building of the White Star liners. Thomas Andrews, the head designer, was Lord Pirrie's nephew.

The concrete slipway of the South Yard in Belfast was made 4.5 feet (1.5 m) thick to support the massive weight of the hulls.

Harland & Wolff's South Yard, Belfast

WHITE STAR
ROYAL MAIL STEAMER
"OLYMPIC"

Shipyard workers

The shipyard employed around 10,000 people, including skilled engineers and specialist workers, such as boilermakers and riveters. Others were craftsmen who worked on the luxurious fixtures and fittings.

Horse-drawn transport delivered heavy materials.

Steel plates up to 1.5 inches (3.8 cm) thick were stacked in the yard.

Crow's nest for the lookout

Wheelhouse

Bridge

Forecastle deck

RMS Titanic

RMS *Titanic* was designed for luxury and passenger comfort, rather than speed. She was longer than RMS *Mauretania*, but not nearly as fast.

BUILDER: HARLAND AND WOLFF

OWNER: WHITE STAR LINE

LAUNCHED: MAY 31, 1911

LENGTH: 882.75 FT (269 M)

BEAM: 92 FT (28 M)

SPEED: 23 KNOTS (26 MPH / 42 KM/H)

CAPACITY: 3,547 (2,687 PASSENGERS / 860 CREW)

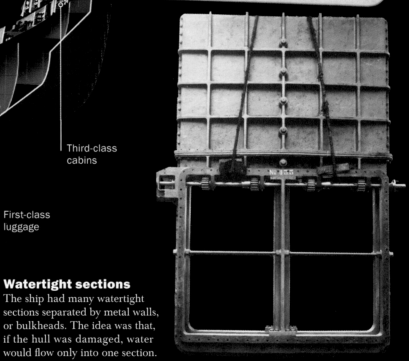

Third-class cabins

Post office

First-class luggage

Coal storage

First-class promenade

Turkish baths

Swimming pool

Watertight sections

The ship had many watertight sections separated by metal walls, or bulkheads. The idea was that, if the hull was damaged, water would flow only into one section.

TITANIC'S PROPULSION SYSTEM

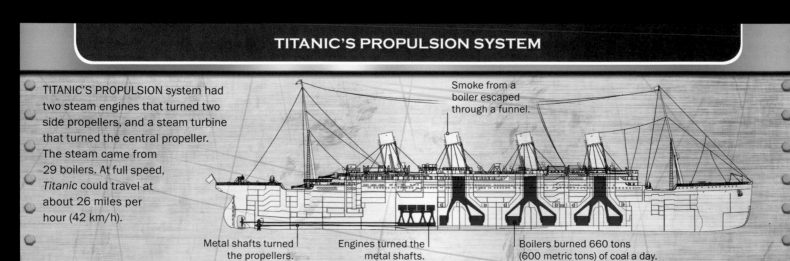

TITANIC'S PROPULSION system had two steam engines that turned two side propellers, and a steam turbine that turned the central propeller. The steam came from 29 boilers. At full speed, *Titanic* could travel at about 26 miles per hour (42 km/h).

Smoke from a boiler escaped through a funnel.

Metal shafts turned the propellers.

Engines turned the metal shafts.

Boilers burned 660 tons (600 metric tons) of coal a day.

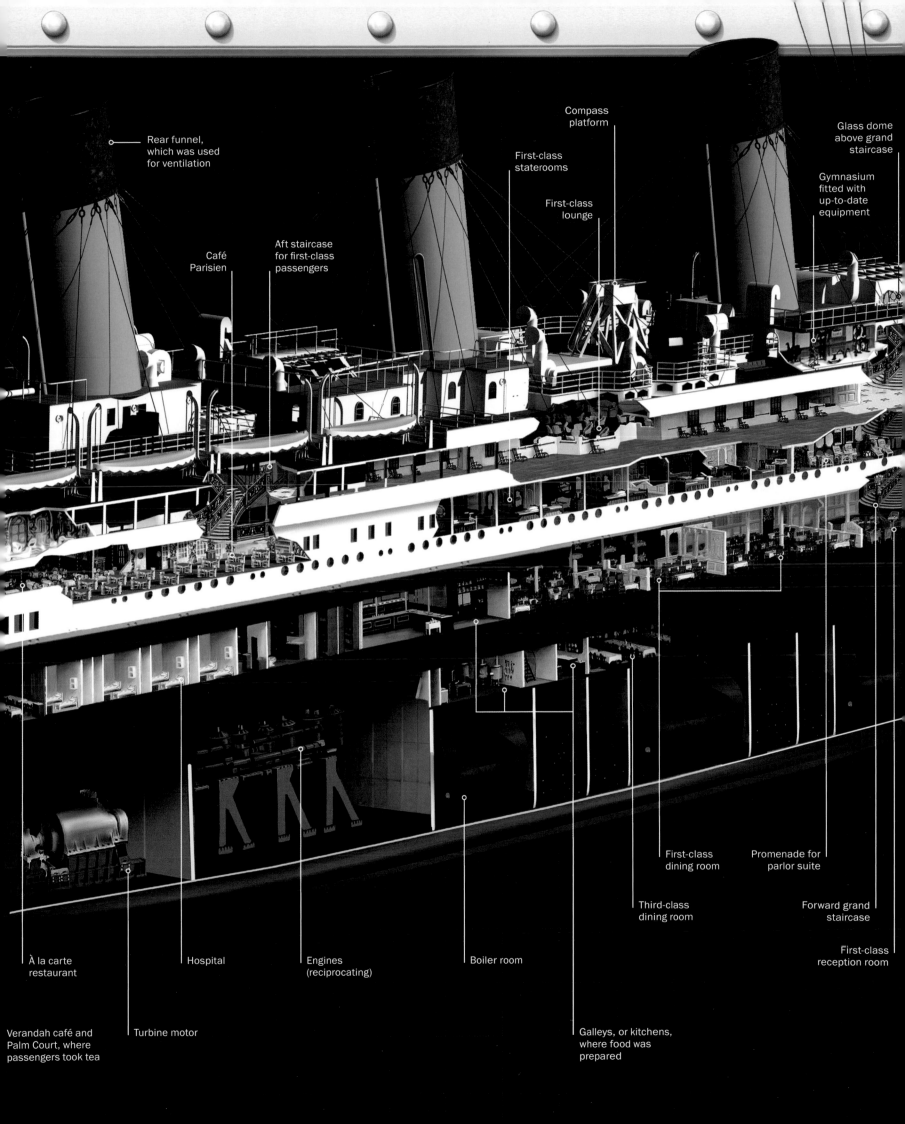

Rear funnel, which was used for ventilation

Compass platform

First-class staterooms

Glass dome above grand staircase

First-class lounge

Gymnasium fitted with up-to-date equipment

Café Parisien

Aft staircase for first-class passengers

First-class dining room

Promenade for parlor suite

Third-class dining room

Forward grand staircase

First-class reception room

À la carte restaurant

Hospital

Engines (reciprocating)

Boiler room

Verandah café and Palm Court, where passengers took tea

Turbine motor

Galleys, or kitchens, where food was prepared

BIRTH OF A TITAN

IN EARLY 1909 THE HARLAND AND WOLFF shipyard in Belfast was buzzing with the news that construction of the world's largest liner had begun. The shipyard had recently been modernized, with the addition of special dry docks to take *Titanic* and her sister ship *Olympic*. An army of skilled workers toiled to lay the keel and build the hull of *Titanic*, and then to fit it out with its engines, boilers, funnels, and interiors. The process took about three years.

Titanic's construction took place in several stages. First, the keel was laid, followed by a steel framework covered with steel plates. Then the finished hull was launched and taken to a nearby wharf, where it was fully fitted out to the designers' requirements.

① Laying the keel
The first job was to build, or lay, the keel. This long metal structure ran all along the bottom of the hull, acting as the "spine" of the ship.

Erecting the frame ②
The framework was erected from around 300 steel sections. Each piece of steel was laid on a vast concrete floor and bent into a specific curving shape.

③ Building the inner decks
Steelwork was added inside the framework to support the ship's decks. By 1910 the builders had reached C deck, in the upper part of the vessel.

④ Launching the hull
More than two years after building started, around 100,000 people watched the fully plated hull, the world's biggest floating object, slide slowly down the slipway into the water.

Folding pocket camera from 1912

Loading the boilers

he boilers were lowered carefully to place inside the hull. The steam gines and the turbine were put gether on board.

⑥〉 Lifting the funnels

Each of the four funnels was 62 feet (19 m) tall. An enormous crane on the wharf was needed to lift them onto the ship and to install them into position.

⑦〉 Fitting out the rooms

Once the engineers and fitters had installed all the heavy equipment that was needed to power *Titanic*, the many rooms on board were fitted out.

⑧〉 Attaching the propellers

The three propellers were made of cast bronze. The two outer propellers, which were the largest, were about four times the height of a man.

LOADING THE SHIP

BEFORE ANY PASSENGERS BOARDED *Titanic*, a small army of people loaded up the vessel with all the supplies that were needed for the journey. Many other items of cargo—some quite strange—belonged to the passengers. *Titanic*'s cargo included everything from a complete Renault car to boxes of pens, feathers, cameras, and candles. Everything had to be lowered carefully into the hold and stacked securely.

SUPPLIES FOR THE JOURNEY

Feeding the passengers and the crew required a staggering amount of food and drink. There were 75,000 pounds (34,019 kg) of fresh meat, 40,000 eggs, 10,000 pounds (4,530 kg) of sugar, and 7,000 heads of lettuce. Loading all this onto the ship was an enormous task.

CLASSES OF DISHES

THE SHIP LEFT SOUTHAMPTON with around 56,700 items of dishware aboard, most of it specially made for *Titanic*. The plates, bowls, cups, and saucers used by the people in third class were very plain compared with the high-quality, gold-decorated tableware that first-class passengers used.

Plates recovered from the seabed

200 barrels of flour

6,000 pounds (2,721 kg) butter

40 tons (36,000 kg) of potatoes

11,000 pounds (4,990 kg) of fresh fish

40,000 eggs

20,000 bottles of beer and 1,500 bottles of wine

THIS WAY UP

5 baby grand pianos

2,200 pounds (997 kg) of coffee and 800 pounds (363 kg) of tea

CURSED CARGO

THERE IS A STORY about a cursed Egyptian mummy that was taken on board *Titanic* and brought about the disaster. The tale is untrue—there was no mummy on the ship. The story may be linked to another supposedly cursed mummy that is kept at London's British Museum.

Egyptian coffin containing a mummy

36,000 oranges and 16,000 lemons

1,500 gallons (5,680 l) of fresh milk and 1,750 quarts (1,650 l) of ice cream

The tallyman checks the cargo.

75,000 pounds (34,019 kg) of fresh meat

Strange cargo

From soap and champagne to rabbit skins and rubber, *Titanic*'s hold was loaded with a vast array of bizarre cargo:

★ A Renault 35-hp automobile
★ A marmalade machine
★ A crate of china for Tiffany's
★ *La Circasienne Au Bain*, a painting by Blondel
★ Seven parcels of parchment of the Torah
★ Three crates of ancient models for a museum
★ 50 cases of toothpaste
★ 11 bales of rubber
★ A jeweled copy of an illustrated book, *The Rubáiyát* by Omar Khayyám
★ Five baby grand pianos
★ 76 cases of "Dragon's Blood" (a kind of sap from a palm tree used in makeup and printing)
★ 15 crates of rabbit hair
★ A barrel of soil for American Express

COAL SHORTAGE

A NATIONAL MINERS' STRIKE in Britain ended only a few days before *Titanic* sailed. But there was no time to bring in new supplies of coal, so the owners were forced to take coal from other White Star Line ships that were docked at Southampton.

Barge laden with coal

THE VOYAGE BEGINS

O N WEDNESDAY, APRIL 10, 1912, *Titanic* was finally ready to set sail from the wharf at Southampton, England. Nearly one thousand passengers went on board that morning and 885 officers and crew were at their posts. At 9:30 a.m. Bruce Ismay, head of the White Star Line, and naval architect Thomas Andrews came aboard to inspect the ship and by mid-morning all was ready for the departure.

SAYING FAREWELL

As excited onlookers waved farewell from the wharf, powerful tugs pulled *Titanic* away from the dock and into the River Test. The captain gave the order to start her engines and the ship's whistle—the largest ever made—was blown to signal the departure. As she steamed away, she narrowly avoided hitting the ship *New York*.

Poster
Titanic's maiden voyage was advertised in colorful posters.

TITANIC
WHITE STAR LINE
The World's Largest Liners

SOUTHAMPTON ~ NEW YORK
VIA CHERBOURG & QUEENSTOWN

Ports of call
Titanic called at Cherbourg, France, then Queenstown (now Cobh) in Ireland before heading out to the Atlantic.

Queenstown

Southampton

Toward
New York

Cherbourg

Luggage tenders
Titanic anchored between breakwaters off Cherbourg and in the bay off Queenstown because neither port was big enough to take her. Special boats, called tenders, carried passengers and their luggage to the liner. There were two White Star tenders at each port: *Nomadic* and *Traffic* at Cherbourg, with *Ireland* and *America*, shown in the picture below, at Queenstown.

TITANIC

CLOSE TO DISASTER

AS TITANIC WAS LEAVING Southampton, she nearly collided with *New York*, which was docked nearby. Disaster was avoided when *Titanic* reversed her engines and a nearby tug pulled *New York* clear.

The power of the liner's engines sucked *New York* toward her.

New York is pulled away from her berth.

The tugboat *Vulcan*

1. Leaving port
As *Titanic* started to move, her engines created a huge swell, which caused *New York* to break her moorings.

2. Near miss
New York was pulled close to the reversing *Titanic*, but *Vulcan* and another tug kept the ships from colliding.

3. All's well
The crew of both tugs managed to pull *New York* clear and *Titanic* continued on her maiden voyage.

The tall funnels kept the smoke and fumes away from passengers on the decks below.

Passengers and crew watched from the decks.

Waving her off
Many people, including friends and family of the passengers, waved from the harbor's edge.

WHITE STAR LINE

YOUR ATTENTION IS SPECIALLY DIRECTED TO THE CONDITIONS OF TRANSPORTATION IN THE ENCLOSED CONTRACT.

THE COMPANY'S LIABILITY FOR BAGGAGE IS STRICTLY LIMITED, BUT PASSENGERS CAN PROTECT THEMSELVES BY INSURANCE.

First-Class Passenger Ticket per Steamship *Titanic*

SAILING FROM
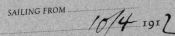
10/4 1912

An unused ticket
This ticket belonged to Reverend Holden, who was unable to sail because his wife was ill.

ON THE BRIDGE

THE BRIDGE, A HIGH PLATFORM open at the sides and with a long window looking out over the bow, was the nerve center of *Titanic*. Several officers and other seamen stood there, keeping watch on the view ahead, giving orders to the engine room, and charting the vessel's course. Telephones and devices called telegraphs linked the bridge to other parts of the ship. There were controls to open and close the vessel's watertight doors and to send whistle signals during fog.

TITANIC *Tales*
CAPTAIN EDWARD JOHN SMITH

Captain Edward John Smith had worked for the White Star Line for more than 30 years. By 1912 he was 60 years old and, as White Star's senior captain, had commanded large ships such as *Baltic*. He was hoping to retire after his voyage on *Titanic*, but perished in the sinking.

Captain Edward John Smith

Officers on the bridge used the main engine telegraph to send orders to the engine room—for example, to change speed or to stop the ship.

The all-important ship's compass was kept in a stand called a binnacle, which was located at the center of the bridge.

THE BRIDGE TELEGRAPH

A CREW MEMBER on the bridge turned a handle on a dial so that it pointed to the order being sent. A series of wires linked this telegraph to the dial on a similar one elsewhere on the ship, such as the engine room. Here, a crew member could read the order that had been sent.

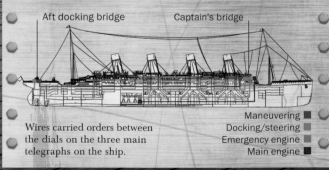

Aft docking bridge   Captain's bridge

Wires carried orders between the dials on the three main telegraphs on the ship.

Maneuvering ■
Docking/steering ■
Emergency engine ■
Main engine ■

The docking telegraph linked the main bridge with the aft bridge near the stern. It was used when the ship entered or left a port.

This wheel was used for steering the ship during fair weather and in a port.

THE CROW'S NEST LOOKOUT

THE CROW'S NEST was a platform on the forward mast, about 50 feet (15.25 m) above the forecastle deck and reached by an iron ladder. On the evening of the collision, the men in the crow's nest had been ordered to keep a sharp lookout for ice.

Fred Fleet, the lookout

The crow's nest

The bridge

Fred Fleet and Reginald Lee in the crow's nest

An officer kept watch on the water ahead with a pair of powerful binoculars.

This maneuvering telegraph received messages about docking movements, or maneuvers, from the aft bridge near the stern.

An officer checks the navigation charts on the chart table.

The captain often came to the bridge, where he gave orders and kept in touch with his officers.

A second main engine telegraph

AMONG THE BOILERS

TITANIC'S ENGINES WORKED by steam power, which was created in a series of 29 boilers. Men shoveled coal into each of these boilers, where it was burned and the heat produced boiling water and turned it into steam. A team of 176 firemen, working in shifts, tended the boilers. Their job was to keep the fires in the boiler furnaces continuously supplied with coal and to watch the fires constantly to make sure that they were burning at the correct rate.

This was hard work—in blistering heat, the team shoveled hundreds of tons of coal every day. But it was also a highly skilled job, because firemen had to lay the coal evenly in the furnaces to make sure it burned properly. It was also important to feed the furnaces quickly as they lost heat when their doors were open.

Stoking the boilers

The firemen shoveled masses of coal into the three furnaces of each boiler. They often worked in shifts lasting four hours. The heat in the boiler room was intense and usually reached 120°F (50°C).

STOKERS

MOST OF TITANIC'S hard-working firemen came from Southampton, on England's south coast, where many people worked in the shipping industry. They were known as stokers because they stoked the furnaces in the boilers with coal. They were tough, strong men with plenty of stamina, and many knew one another already because they had worked together on other ships. Few of the stokers survived the disaster.

One stoker, known only as Turner, is said to be "the man who could not be drowned" because he survived several disasters, such as *Lusitania* and *Titanic*. But he is not listed on *Titanic*'s crew so his story seems to be a myth.

POWERING TITANIC

MOST OF TITANIC'S POWER came from two enormous main engines. They were running all the time and consumed vast amounts of coal and water.

Did you know:
★ Each main engine created around 16,000 horsepower (11,930 kW), equivalent to about 100 medium-sized family cars.
★ Each main engine weighed around 1,100 tons (1,000 t) and was about 30 feet (9 m) tall—roughly the height of a three-story house.
★ *Titanic* carried about 8,800 tons (8,000 t) of coal to fuel the engines on the Atlantic crossing.

The engine room of an Olympic-class liner

THE LAP OF LUXURY

EXPERIENCED SEA TRAVELERS were impressed with the luxury on board *Titanic*—some even said the ship was like a palace. First-class passengers were especially impressed by the spacious reception and dining areas where they could relax and eat in five-star surroundings. These rooms were furnished with luxurious carpets and curtains, and beautifully decorated with fine wood paneling and rich plasterwork in the ceilings.

NOTHING BUT THE BEST

First-class passengers enjoyed luxury accommodations that reminded them more of the rooms in a grand hotel or stately home than the cramped cabins on board many other ships. Their bathrooms were equipped with hot and cold running water, and their sitting rooms, with portholes that could be opened for ventilation, had the best-quality furniture. Some passengers even had their own private promenade deck.

The first-class areas

Most of the first-class staterooms and reception rooms were in the middle of the ship, close to the two grand staircases.

- First-class staircases
- Dining room
- Spa area
- Cafés
- Lounge areas
- First-class cabins

STAIRCASE R.M.S. TITANIC

The grand staircase

This oak-paneled staircase was decorated with statues and carvings and had iron balustrades. A big glass dome let in daylight to add to the lights from brass fittings on the walls and ceilings.

Café Parisien

This café was a sunlit room with windows along one long side. People sat at small tables in a less formal style than in the main dining room.

The first-class dining room

This was the largest room on the ship. It measured about 114 feet (35 m) in length and could seat more than 500 people.

FIRST CLASS
7
WHITE STAR LINE

A pin badge worn by a first-class cabin steward

First-class cabins

First-class passengers stayed in staterooms that had big, comfortable beds. The richest passengers paid for an entire suite of rooms, with bedrooms (near right and far right) and even a private promenade deck (below right) that was open to the air.

First-class lounge

First-class passengers relaxed in a lounge (above), where they read and wrote letters in a quiet, comfortable atmosphere. The room was particularly popular with women, whereas men congregated in the ship's smoking rooms.

Titanic's spa facilities

Passengers swam in the swimming pool or used the gymnasium's modern equipment, such as the rowing machine and electric camel. Afterward, they could relax in the luxurious Turkish bath.

Turkish bath

Gymnasium

Swimming pool

A GRAND EVENING

THE HIGHLIGHT ON BOARD *Titanic* was the evening meal. In first class this was a huge meal with many courses, and the food was cooked by highly skilled chefs and served with the best wines. Dinner was a grand and glittering occasion, with the passengers dressed in their best evening clothes. It was a chance to catch up with old friends, make new acquaintances, and talk about what had happened on board during the day.

GATHERING TOGETHER

A little while before dinner the first-class passengers left their staterooms and luxury cabins, descended the grand staircase, and gathered in the reception area next to the dining room. Here they drank cocktails with Captain Smith and perhaps a senior officer, too.

⚓ TITANIC *Tales* ⚓

JOHN AND MADELEINE ASTOR

The Astors were one of the wealthiest couples on board *Titanic*. Born into a rich family, John Astor had made a fortune in the property business with developments such as New York's Waldorf Astoria Hotel. His marriage to 18-year-old Madeleine Force caused a huge scandal.

John and Madeleine Astor

⚓ TITANIC *Tales* ⚓

MARGARET "MOLLY" BROWN

Margaret came from a poor family in America, but her husband made a great deal of money in the mining industry in Colorado. Margaret used her money to fund children's and women's charities. She also traveled widely, making many trips around the world.

Margaret Brown

Beautiful jewelry

ealthy women wore their
est jewelry, which sparkled
th gems such as rubies,
amonds, and sapphires.

TITANIC Tales
LADY DUFF GORDON

Lucy Duff Gordon, the wife of
Scottish landowner Sir Cosmo
Duff Gordon, had a successful career
as a fashion designer under the name
of "Lucile." She was famous for the
designs of her evening wear and was
said to be one of the most elegant
women on *Titanic*.

Lucy Duff Gordon

Beautiful gowns

Dressing for dinner gave the
first-class women passengers
the opportunity to show off
their most beautiful gowns.

R.M.S. TITANIC

APRIL 10, 1912.

Hors d'Œuvre Variés

Consommé Réjane   Crème Reine Margot

Turbot, Sauce Homard
Whitebait

Mutton Cutlets & Green Peas
Suprême of Chicken à la Stanley

Sirloin of Beef, Château Potatoes
Roast Duckling, Apple Sauce
Fillet of Veal & Braised Ham

Cauliflower   Spinach
Boiled Rice
Bovin & Boiled New Potatoes

Plover on Toast & Cress
Salad

Pudding Sans Souci
Charlotte Colville
Granvilles

French Ice Cream

Meals to remember

First-class passengers enjoyed the kind
of food served at the best restaurants.
Hors d'oeuvres, soup, and fish were
followed by delicious meats (including
unusual types, such as a bird called
a plover) with sauces and vegetables.

OTHER CLASSES

ABOUT THREE-QUARTERS of *Titanic*'s passengers traveled second or third class. They paid less for their tickets and their facilities were not as luxurious as those in first class. Second-class travelers had comfortable cabins and spacious public rooms, and they shared some first-class facilities, such as the library. Third-class passengers, by contrast, often slept six to a cabin, and they had only a general room, a smoking room for the men, and limited areas on deck.

A HIGH STANDARD

The White Star Line boasted that second class on *Titanic* was as luxurious as first class on most other liners. Those traveling second class had their own dining room and promenade deck, where they could relax and chat with fellow passengers.

Second-class cabin
Cabins in second class had two or four berths with a curtain around them. They did not have hot and cold running water and passengers had to use communal bathrooms.

TITANIC *Tales*
TITANIC ORPHANS

French brothers Michel and Edmond Navratil, aged 3 and 2, were traveling with their father, also named Michel, who died in the sinking. The boys escaped in collapsible lifeboat D and became known as the "Titanic orphans." They later returned to France to live with their mother.

Michel and Edmond Navratil

LIFE IN STEERAGE

...cial life in third class—also known as steerage—centered ...the general room, where people sat, talked, and made ...eir own entertainment. Many of the 710 passengers in ...ird class came from Ireland and were emigrating to America to start a new life. A gathering of musicians played traditional Irish music on the piano, fiddle, drum, and uilleann pipes, while others danced and talked.

INSPECTION AND IMMIGRATION

PASSENGERS IN THIRD CLASS were poor people who traveled with little luggage. Each carried a green inspection card that showed their name, the last country where they lived, the name of the ship, and the port from which it departed. This was designed to help the immigration authorities when the passengers arrived in New York.

Third-class inspection card

WRITING HOME

EVEN FOR PASSENGERS used to sea travel, an exciting voyage on the world's greatest liner was the trip of a lifetime. Many of the passengers were eager to tell their friends all about it. They sat in the café or library writing letters home, getting their impressions of their wonderful journey down on paper while everything was still fresh in the mind. Few letters from the ship have survived because most of the mail went down during the sinking.

The wireless operator could send messages home.

Exercising in the gymnasium

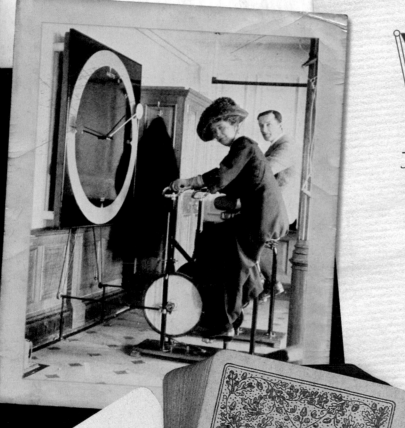

On Board R•M•S• "TITANIC".
April 12, 1912

Dearest Carrie,

We're having a wonderful time on the journey. Our berths are comfortable and we have plenty of space in the cabin, but we spend most of our time in the public rooms and on deck. Jack enjoys the gymnasium and says he's going to buy an exercise bicycle like the one on board when he gets home.

I like the Verandah Café, where I'm sitting now having a delicious cup of tea. Many of the women in First Class go here in the afternoons and I've already made several new friends on board. The dining room is really elegant too. Tonight we're invited to dine at Captain Smith's table— a great honor!

Taking tea by the sea
The Verandah Café and Palm Court had big windows with views overlooking the sea. Here, afternoon tea was served for first-class passengers.

Card games in the lounge
Many passengers whiled away the hours playing card games. At the time, bridge was a popular game with both men and women.

WHITE STAR LINE.

Titanic postcard

The White Star Line had postcards specially printed for the journey. This one shows the grandeur and size of one of the White Star ships at sea.

Taking a walk

Although it was cold in the North Atlantic, passengers liked to take advantage of the long promenade decks to go for a walk. The dogs on board were exercised here too.

WHITE STAR LINE

Playtime on deck

Children went out onto the saloon deck to play in the fresh air. This boy is spinning a wooden top while his father watches.

DREAMS AND VISIONS

ONE OF THE STRANGEST THINGS about *Titanic*'s story is that, in spite of the fact that the ship was very well built, a number of people seem to have predicted the disaster. Some predictions came from people who had thought deeply about the dangers and who worried that transatlantic ocean liners did not carry enough lifeboats. Others came as warnings in dreams or visions, in which passengers floundered in freezing water, or lifeboats drifted across the cold, dark sea.

A novel idea
In his novel *Futility*, published in 1898, Morgan Robertson tells of a huge liner, called *Titan*, which sinks in the Atlantic after hitting an iceberg. Many die because there are not enough lifeboats.

A sense of danger
Frank Adelman, a Seattle violinist, planned to travel home on *Titanic* with his wife. When she had a premonition of danger, they tossed a coin to decide whether to travel on board *Titanic*. Mrs. Adelman won and they took another ship.

Nightmare
Mr. Shepherd was an American traveling in England on business. His wife wrote to him saying she'd had a nightmare in which *Titanic* had sunk, so he changed his plans and returned home on another ship.

A sudden realization
As Blanche Marshall watched *Titanic* leaving Southampton, she grabbed her husband's arm and cried, "That ship's going to sink. I can see hundreds of people struggling in icy water."

BAD OMENS

SUPERSTITIOUS PEOPLE worried about *Titanic* because they saw a number of things connected with it as bad omens. Some of these things were:
- ★ Captain Smith had already had one bad accident. While he was captain of *Olympic*, it collided with HMS *Hawke*.
- ★ At Queenstown, a stoker appeared at the top of the rear funnel and scared the crowd watching on the wharf.
- ★ The ship was not christened in a naming ceremony, although neither were any other White Star liners.
- ★ In the house of a White Star employee, a picture fell to the floor, an event seen as a bad omen among sailors and their families.

The damage to *Olympic* caused by the collision with *Hawke*

The Egyptian palm reader

When the Canadian Fortune family were traveling in Egypt, a palm reader told Alice Fortune that she'd be in danger if she traveled by sea. A few months later the family boarded *Titanic*. She survived with her mother and sisters, but her father and brother were lost.

∽TITANIC *Tales*∽
A TRAGEDY FORETOLD

In 1886 British journalist William Stead published a story as a warning to ship owners. It described how a steamer hit an iceberg in the Atlantic and sank, causing many deaths because there were not enough lifeboats. Stead was on board *Titanic* and died when it sank.

William Stead

A dying girl's vision

On the night of April 14, 1912, Rex Sowden, a Scottish Salvation Army officer, was called to the bedside of a dying girl. She told him about her vision of a huge sinking ship with a man named Wally playing a fiddle and many people drowning.

A black silhouette

Frenchman Michel Navratil traveled on *Titanic* with his two small sons. His wife dreamed a black silhouette handed her a letter saying her husband was dead. He perished, but his sons survived.

Submerged danger
Up to nine-tenths of the ice that makes up an iceberg is below the water's surface. Icebergs therefore pose a huge danger to the submerged part of a ship's hull.

TRAGEDY STRIKES

ON THE NIGHT OF APRIL 14, 1912, almost 10 hours after *Titanic*'s radio operator had heard the first warning of ice, the ship's lookout saw the iceberg from the crow's nest. Officers on the bridge turned the ship slightly, but it was not enough to avoid a collision. At first the passengers who were awake stayed calm because they thought the ship was unsinkable. But soon they felt vibrations and heard a thunder-like rumble as the vessel scraped along the ice. As the crew tried to pump out the water coming on board, many passengers, woken by the noise, got dressed and left their cabins to find out what was going on.

TOO MUCH DAMAGE

AS THE SHIP SCRAPED the side of the iceberg, a series of holes opened up in the starboard side of the hull. Water entered five watertight compartments—one too many for *Titanic*, which would have stayed afloat with four flooded.

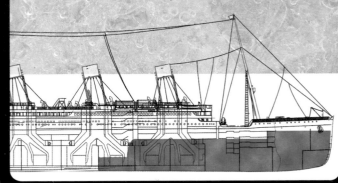

TIMELINE
13:42 – 23:53
(BRIDGE TIME)

The time on board the ship is called Bridge Time. It is adjusted to correspond to local time zones as the ship moves across the ocean.

13:42 (APRIL 14)

The commander of *Baltic* sends a radio report of large quantities of ice in the area to which *Titanic* is sailing.

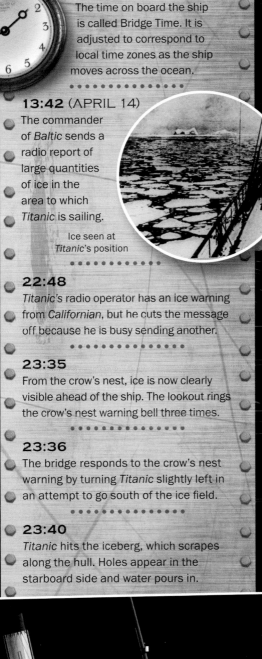

Ice seen at *Titanic*'s position

22:48

Titanic's radio operator has an ice warning from *Californian*, but he cuts the message off because he is busy sending another.

23:35

From the crow's nest, ice is now clearly visible ahead of the ship. The lookout rings the crow's nest warning bell three times.

23:36

The bridge responds to the crow's nest warning by turning *Titanic* slightly left in an attempt to go south of the ice field.

23:40

Titanic hits the iceberg, which scrapes along the hull. Holes appear in the starboard side and water pours in.

Holes in the hull extended from bow to first funnel

23:53

Captain Smith orders the engines to be stopped for the final time.

...it below the water

...itanic seems to narrowly ...iss the iceberg, but is ...sastrously hit by the ice ...dden below the water.

ABANDON SHIP!

SEVERAL MINUTES AFTER *Titanic* hit the iceberg, Captain Smith realized the ship would probably sink, so he ordered his men to prepare the lifeboats. Many passengers were still in their cabins, unaware of what had happened. Some were even asleep. As crew members raised the alarm, they were more helpful and courteous to first- and second-class passengers. Many third-class passengers, however, were prevented from reaching the decks.

ALL CALM IN FIRST CLASS

Crew members knocked on the doors of first-class cabins on the upper parts of the ship and politely asked bewildered passengers to put on warm coats and their life jackets, and to calmly report on deck.

LIFE JACKETS

TITANIC HAD ENOUGH LIFE JACKETS for everyone on board. The jackets had pieces of cork sewn into them to make them float. The cork was heavy and hard—some people who jumped into the water were hit by the pieces of cork, causing injuries such as a broken jaw.

Canvas straps were used to fasten a life jacket.

∼TITANIC *Tales*∼
WILLIAM MURDOCH

First Officer William Murdoch was ordered to send all the first-class passengers on deck and to supervise the lifeboats on the starboard side of the ship. He managed to launch 10 boats, carrying around three-quarters of those who survived, before he went down with the ship.

Lieutenant William McMaster Murdoch RNR

PANIC IN THIRD CLASS

Many third-class passengers were staying in berths just above the iceberg's point of impact and water was already gushing in. As frightened passengers tried to escape up to the decks, their way was blocked by a steel grill, manned by stony-faced pursers.

TIMELINE
23:53 – 00:25
(BRIDGE TIME)

As the lifeboats were being prepared, crew members helped the passengers, while key personnel kept the ship's operations going.

23:53
Captain Smith orders Chief Officer Wilde to begin preparing the lifeboats.

Chief Officer Henry Tingle Wilde Jr.

00:00 (APRIL 15)
Some crew help passengers put on their life jackets; others stay at their posts in the engine rooms or radio room.

Stokers try to escape the flooding engine room.

00:07
Deep in the ship, a boiler is flooded and water rises 8 feet (2.4 m) over the boiler's stoker plates.

00:07
Officers order members of the crew to assist passengers with their life jackets and move them to the boat decks.

00:19
Captain Smith gives the order for the lifeboats to be launched, and the evacuation of the ship begins.

00:25
Electricians get the lights in the ship's boiler room working again after 15 minutes of darkness.

LAUNCHING THE LIFEBOATS

THE 16 WOODEN LIFEBOATS were stowed on the boat deck, with the four collapsibles nearby. Launching involved attaching the boats to the davits, loading them with people, and lowering them steadily down to the water.

FORE

2 D B A C 1

Collapsible B, the last lifeboat to leave

4 6 8 7 5 3

Starboard 7, the first lifeboat to leave

PORT

STARBOARD

10 12 14 16 15 13 11 9

Port 16 was commanded by Harold Lowe

AFT

"A" and "B" collapsible lifeboats were stacked above the boat deck.

ESCAPE

AS THE LIFEBOATS were made ready, women and children were offered the first seats, according to the custom of the time. This is why so many of those who were rescued from the sinking ship were women, along with some of the ship's crew who rowed the boats, and a few male passengers who took their chance to escape. *Titanic* had 20 lifeboats (16 wooden boats and 4 collapsible craft made of canvas), which together could hold up to 1,178 people. Although this was only just over half of those on board the ship, it was quite normal for the period—large liners were not expected to sink.

In midair
As the crew lowered a lifeboat, the terrified passengers were suspended about 60 feet (18 m) above the water,

TIMELINE
00:26 – 01:41
(BRIDGE TIME)

The lifeboats, including two collapsibles, were launched from port and starboard sides over a period of one hour and 15 minutes.

00:26

Lifeboat No. 7 is launched first, with actress Dorothy Gibson among its 28 passengers.

Dorothy Gibson

00:35

Lifeboat No. 5 is launched. Henry Frauenthal, with his wife and brother, jump in as it's lowered, injuring a woman.

00:42

Lifeboat No. 1 is launched with only 12 passengers, including Sir Cosmo and Lady Duff Gordon, on board.

01:36

Collapsible lifeboat C is launched with 44 on board, including Bruce Ismay, who is later criticized for leaving his ship.

A passenger jumps into a passing lifeboat.

01:41

Collapsible lifeboat D is launched with 22 on board. Hugh Woolner and Lt. Steffanson leap in as it passes A deck.

Boats away

When a lifeboat had safely reached the water, one of the crew members on board signaled to the man on deck that he was detaching the ropes and was ready to sail away.

FACING THE INEVITABLE

DURING THE SHIP'S FINAL MINUTES, the last few lifeboats were made ready and loaded, but those who remained were still huddled together on the boat deck. Many were men, and each one was facing the inevitable thought that they would probably go down with the ship. They realized that there was almost no chance of getting on board one of the lifeboats, even though they saw that some were being launched half full because the ship's officers enforced the "women and children first" rule very strictly. In spite of this, the remaining passengers managed to keep calm.

Women and children
While the men waited on deck, the wooden lifeboats were filled with women and children under the strict supervision of a loading officer.

Take your turn
Officers on deck had a hard time controlling the excited passengers, especially when men from third class tried to get on board a lifeboat.

Final farewell
Many of the remaining men said goodbye to their loved ones while the ship's musicians played on until the very end.

TITANIC *Tales*
CHARLES LIGHTOLLER

Second Officer Charles Lightoller was in charge of launching lifeboats on the port side of *Titanic*. At the end, when the ship went down, he jumped into the water and managed to grab hold of the upturned collapsible lifeboat B. He was the most senior officer to survive *Titanic*'s sinking.

Charles Herbert Lightoller

~TITANIC *Tales* ~
WALLY HARTLEY

Bandmaster and violinist Wallace Hartley joined the White Star Line for *Titanic*'s maiden voyage. He led a quintet that played during evening meals, at onboard concerts, and during religious services. Like his fellow musicians, he went down with the ship.

Wally played lead violin in his quintet.

The band plays on
Bandleader Wally Hartley and the musicians from his quintet joined the ship's trio to play on the boat deck to help people remain calm.

TIMELINE
01:41 — 01:51
(BRIDGE TIME)

As the ship was going down, it listed to port and tipped up dramatically, making it hard for passengers and crew to keep upright.

01:41
Collapsible lifeboat D is launched from the port side; this is the last boat to be successfully launched.

01:43
As *Titanic* rolls more to port, Captain Smith tries to steady it by sending people on the port side to join others on the starboard side of the deck.

01:49
Titanic's hull begins to break up and collapsible lifeboat B washes off the deck before anyone can get into it.

01:50
Funnel No. 1 collapses on the port side of the ship, causing a wave that overturns collapsible lifeboat B.

01:50
Kitchen worker John Collins is swept overboard by water; a baby he is carrying is washed from his arms.

August grabs a deck chair.

01:51
Ship's barber August Weikman, who has been washed off deck, swims toward some floating deck chairs.

TITANIC SINKS

IN HER FINAL FEW MOMENTS *Titanic* tipped up in the water and the hull broke apart. As she went down, a few of those who were still on board jumped into the ocean, where some kept afloat by clinging to wreckage or swam to the safety of the lifeboats. Many survivors looked on in horror from the lifeboats, as they bobbed about in the ocean. Their lives were still uncertain in the freezing cold night as they hoped and prayed for rescue.

THE FINAL MOMENTS
Terrified passengers left on the liner crowded toward the stern, as it stayed above the water longest. Many were second- and third-class passengers, who drowned as the ship disappeared.

Down by the head
With the forward part of the ship flooded, her nose was pulled under the water, submerging the bridge and officers' quarters.

About two-thirds of the ship submerged.

The angle increases
The weight of the water inside the ship pulled the vessel still deeper, leaving the stern sticking high out of the water.

The stern returned toward the water.

The breakup
The huge stresses of the sinking caused the ship to break in two between the third and fourth funnels.

To the bottom
The ship's bow sank quickly to the bottom, followed by a mass of debris, including boilers, funnels, and bits of the broken hull.

⟳ TITANIC *Tales* ⟳
MARGARET "MOLLY" BROWN

In Lifeboat No. 6, Quartermaster Robert Hichens refused Margaret Brown's plea to look for survivors. So she urged other women to take oars and row, and Hichens gave in. She became known as "the unsinkable Molly Brown."

American women's rights campaigner Margaret Brown

⟳ TITANIC *Tales* ⟳
LIFEBOAT HERO

Harold Lowe was the ship's officer in charge of Lifeboat No. 14. Hearing the screams of dying passengers in the water, he transferred people from his lifeboat into others, then rowed back and saved a few struggling survivors from the ocean and also from a sinking lifeboat.

Harold Lowe

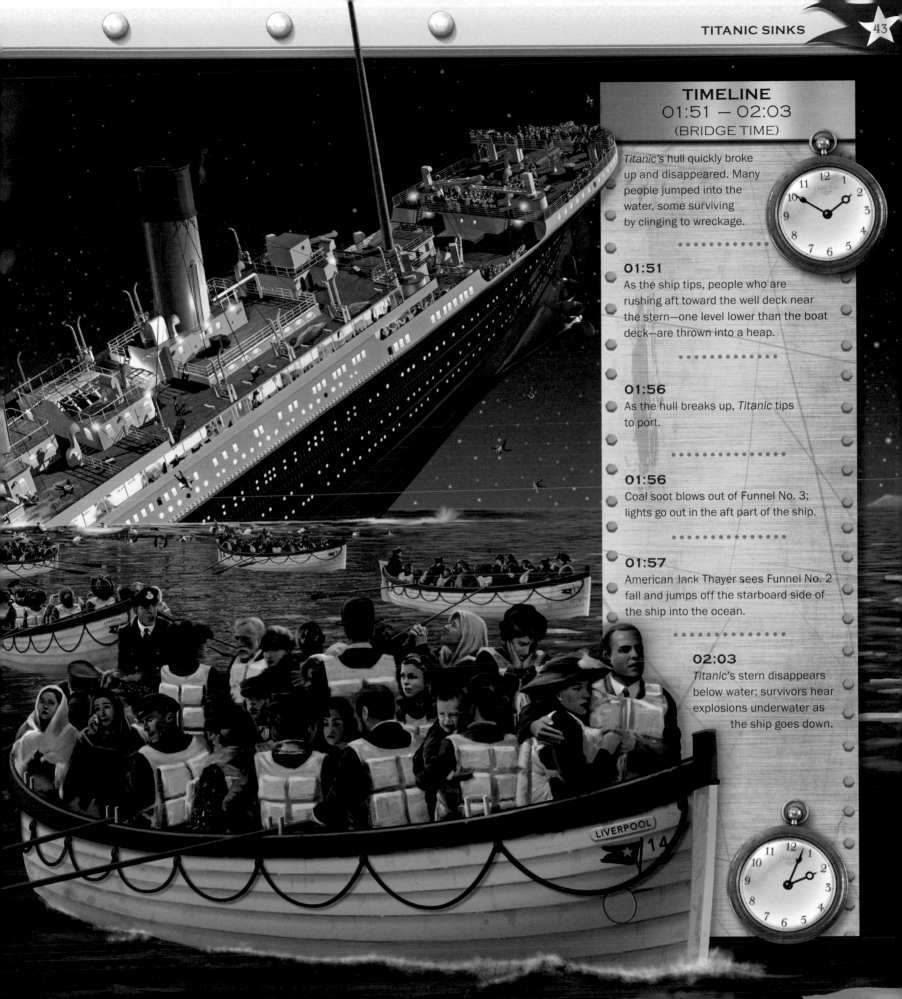

TIMELINE
01:51 — 02:03
(BRIDGE TIME)

Titanic's hull quickly broke up and disappeared. Many people jumped into the water, some surviving by clinging to wreckage.

01:51
As the ship tips, people who are rushing aft toward the well deck near the stern—one level lower than the boat deck—are thrown into a heap.

01:56
As the hull breaks up, *Titanic* tips to port.

01:56
Coal soot blows out of Funnel No. 3; lights go out in the aft part of the ship.

01:57
American Jack Thayer sees Funnel No. 2 fall and jumps off the starboard side of the ship into the ocean.

02:03
Titanic's stern disappears below water; survivors hear explosions underwater as the ship goes down.

LIVERPOOL
14

All at sea
Crew members rowed the lifeboats away from where *Titanic* had gone down in the hope of reaching the safety of a passing ship.

Deliveranc
As one of th
lifeboats reache
Carpathia, passenge
prepared to climb
ladders to the dec

RESCUE

THE NEAREST SHIP to the stricken *Titanic* was a Cunard liner, RMS *Carpathia*. This ship was about 58 miles (93 km) away and changed its course, sailing through the dangerous ice field, to look for survivors. When *Carpathia* arrived where its captain thought *Titanic* should be, the vast ship had vanished and there was nothing to be seen. Then a crew member in Lifeboat No. 2 saw a flare. Soon, other lifeboats made for *Carpathia* and survivors climbed aboard, telling the shocked crew that *Titanic* had sunk.

TIMELINE
03:30 – 21:25
(NEW YORK TIME)

Carpathia spent several hours in the area where *Titanic* sank, picking up the lifeboats and taking all the survivors on board.

03:30
Many survivors in the lifeboats see rockets, fired at 15-minute intervals by the crew of *Carpathia*.

04:32
Survivors in Lifeboat No. 2 are the first to be picked up by *Carpathia*.

06:02
Another ship, *Californian*, joins *Carpathia* to help with the rescue of survivors.

06:32
Lifeboat No. 12—the last lifeboat to be rescued—draws alongside *Carpathia*. More than 70 survivors climb aboard. Lightoller is the last survivor of all to board.

08:00
Carpathia leaves the area and steams toward New York with 705 survivors on board. Bruce Ismay radios New York's White Star office with the news that *Titanic* has sunk.

21:25 (APRIL 18)
Carpathia finally docks at New York in front of many thousands of people.

afe at last
e survivors gathered on e deck of *Carpathia*. Many scovered that other family embers had not reached e safety of the ship.

Frostbitten feet
Radio operator Harold Bride had to be helped from *Carpathia* because his feet were badly frostbitten after he spent time in the ice-cold water.

◦◦ TITANIC *Tales* ◦◦
CARPATHIA TO THE RESCUE

When *Carpathia*'s radio operator heard *Titanic*'s distress signal, her captain set a course toward the sinking ship. Immediately, first-aid stations, hot drinks, and blankets were made ready. *Carpathia* eventually took 705 survivors on board.

Carpathia's Captain, Sir Arthur Henry Rostron

Carpathia enters New York

TITANIC DISASTER
TALES OF SURVIVAL AND LOSS

THE STORY OF APRIL 14, 1912, is remembered as a great tragedy, but in reality there were more than 2,000 separate stories of individuals, from small children to elderly men and women, who came face to face with death. People reacted in all kinds of ways, but many of the men kept rigidly to the traditional rule of "women and children first," effectively giving up their lives so that their womenfolk could get into the lifeboats and away to safety. These men, together with the crew members who helped care for female passengers shivering and frightened on deck, are now remembered as heroes.

WHITE STAR BOSS ISMAY SURVIVES

Chairman of the White Star Line, Bruce Ismay, was rescued in collapsible lifeboat C. Many people thought that, as owner, he should have stayed on board the sinking ship, and gone down with her. They even called him a coward. But others disagreed, saying he had first helped to save the lives of many women and children.

DID BRIBERY ENSURE SIR COSMO'S SAFETY?

Sir Cosmo Duff Gordon, a British businessman, and his wife Lucy survived the sinking after they climbed into Lifeboat No. 1. Even though it could have taken many people, this lifeboat put to sea with only 12, and seven of them were crew. Some critics have accused Duff Gordon of bribing the crew of the lifeboat to leave as quickly as possible, but a public inquiry found no evidence of bribery.

THE SURVIVAL OF TITANIC'S STEWARDESSES

The 20 stewardesses on *Titanic* worked as maids, mostly in the first-class cabins and staterooms. Two worked in the Turkish baths. When *Titanic* began to sink, the stewardesses helped the women passengers on deck, comforting them and handing out blankets to keep them warm. Most of the stewardesses at first refused to get into the lifeboats. They said they had work to do on deck and thought they should give priority to the women passengers and children. But Bruce Ismay, the ship's boss, ordered them to get into the lifeboats and so 18 of the stewardesses were rescued.

"You are women, and I wish you would get in." **BRUCE ISMAY**

TUESDAY APRIL 23, 1912

TANIC'S TINIEST URVIVOR

anic's youngest survivor was llvina Dean, a nine-week-old by who was traveling with her rents and her brother Bertram Kansas in the United States. t Mr. Dean perished in the saster, so Millvina, Bertram, d their mother returned to gland. Millvina would live to the e old age of 97 and become *anic*'s longest-lived survivor.

TYCOON GOES DOWN WITH SHIP

Benjamin Guggenheim was one of the richest businessmen in America. He ran a large company that owned mines and manufactured mining machinery. Guggenheim was returning home on *Titanic* from a holiday in Europe with his secretary and his mistress. His wife and their three daughters had stayed at home in New York.

DOING HIS DUTY

When he realized that the ship was sinking, the tycoon and his secretary put on their best evening clothes and went on deck to help the women and children into the lifeboats. He asked a member of the crew that if he should die his wife should be told, "I've done my best in doing my duty." Strictly following the "women and children first" rule, Guggenheim and his secretary went down with the ship.

"We've dressed up in our best and are prepared to go down like gentlemen."

BENJAMIN GUGGENHEIM

MILLIONAIRE GIVES UP PLACE

Millionaire property developer, writer, and inventor John Jacob Astor was traveling home with his new young wife, Madeleine, who was pregnant. He helped her climb into a lifeboat, said goodbye, and then watched the boat sail away. Hours later, he had drowned.

MAN OF FAITH AND PRAYER

Father Thomas Byles was a British Catholic priest who was sailing to New York to officiate at the wedding of his young brother, William. On Sunday morning he celebrated mass, first in second class and then in third class. When the ship struck the iceberg, he helped women and children into the lifeboats, heard confessions, and prayed with those who were left on the ship and facing the inevitable. He refused the offer of a place in a lifeboat and was drowned.

WHO SURVIVED THAT TERRIBLE NIGHT?

Women and children survived the disaster in greater numbers than men, because they were first into the lifeboats. The statistics of those who survived, shown here, also tell how people in first and second class had a better chance of survival than the passengers in third class. Among the crew, many more women than men escaped the sinking vessel.

97%
1ST/2ND CLASS
(one child died)

34%
3RD CLASS

CHILD PASSENGERS

33%
ST CLASS

16%
RD CLASS

8%
2ND CLASS

MALE PASSENGERS

97%
1ST CLASS

86%
2ND CLASS

46%
3RD CLASS

FEMALE PASSENGERS

87%
FEMALE

22%
MALE

CREW

NEVER AGAIN

THE SHOCKING NEWS of *Titanic*'s sinking made everyone determined to prevent a similar disaster from ever happening again. For a start, ships were equipped with enough lifeboats for all on board. Two inquiries recommended, among other things, that ships slow down in icy conditions and keep their radios permanently turned on so they could pick up distress signals from other vessels.

TWO INQUIRIES

Immediately after the sinking, major inquiries were held in both New York and London. Many people, including the crew, passengers, and White Star boss, gave extraordinary accounts of what happened that fateful night. One important conclusion was that if *Californian*, sailing nearby, had heard *Titanic*'s distress signals, many more people would have been saved.

Ismay gives evidence
Bruce Ismay insisted *Titanic* was not going at full speed. He also said he only got into a lifeboat when no women or children were nearby.

No pay for the crew
Crew members had their pay stop as soon as the ship sank. Some re on gifts of clothes and equipmen

So many mistakes
Several serious mistakes—in the ship's construction, the equipment carried, and the working methods on board—together contributed to the disaster.

Duff Gordon tells his tale
Gordon said he did not bribe the crew of the lifeboat, but gave them money to help replace the gear they had lost.

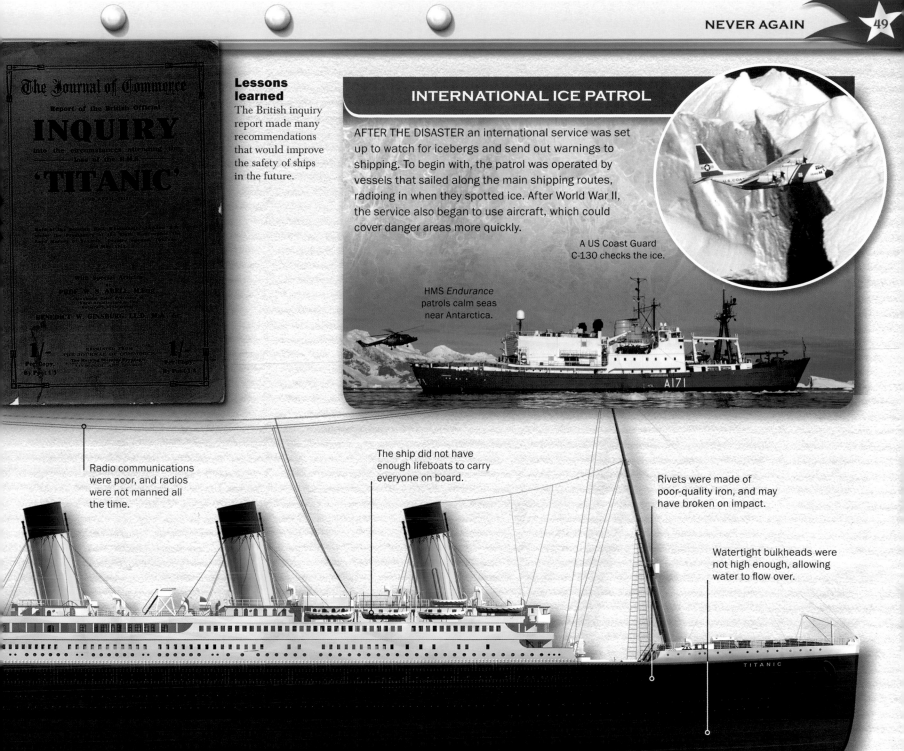

INTERNATIONAL ICE PATROL

AFTER THE DISASTER an international service was set up to watch for icebergs and send out warnings to shipping. To begin with, the patrol was operated by vessels that sailed along the main shipping routes, radioing in when they spotted ice. After World War II, the service also began to use aircraft, which could cover danger areas more quickly.

A US Coast Guard C-130 checks the ice.

HMS *Endurance* patrols calm seas near Antarctica.

A171

Lessons learned
The British inquiry report made many recommendations that would improve the safety of ships in the future.

The Journal of Commerce

Report of the British Official

INQUIRY

into the circumstances attending the loss of the R.M.S.

'TITANIC'

With Special Articles by
PROF. W. S. ABELL, M.Eng.

BENEDICT W. GINSBURG, LL.D., M.A., &c.

1/-
Per Copy.
By Post 1/3

1/-
Per Copy.
By Post 1/3

REPRINTED FROM
THE JOURNAL OF COMMERCE,
The Shipping Newspaper of Liverpool,
LIVERPOOL AND LONDON.

Radio communications were poor, and radios were not manned all the time.

The ship did not have enough lifeboats to carry everyone on board.

Rivets were made of poor-quality iron, and may have broken on impact.

Watertight bulkheads were not high enough, allowing water to flow over.

TITANIC

...fer sailing
...ers such as *Normandie* and ...1S *Queen Mary* ...th launched in ...1930s) had the ...ht number of ...boats and good ...io facilities.

SS *Normandie*

RMS *Queen Mary*

FINDING TITANIC

SOON AFTER THE SINKING, people began to think about finding *Titanic* and exploring the wreck on the seabed. But no one knew exactly where it was, and the deep, ice-cold water made exploration very difficult. Robert Ballard, an American oceanographer and underwater archaeologist, realized that it would be best to use a specially designed submersible craft. In 1985 he and his team explored the ocean floor with a robot submersible called *Argo*, and located the wreck.

GOING CLOSER

In 1986, Ballard's team explored the wreck more closely. They went down in a manned submersible called *Alvin* and used a small robot vessel, *Jason Junior*, to investigate inside the hull. They found the two main parts of the ship and took many photographs of the remains that lay in an area called the "debris field."

The twilight zone
Only a little light reaches the twilight zone, which extends from 650 feet (200 m) down to 3,300 feet (1,000 m).

Alvin and *Jason Junior*
The submersible *Alvin* can carry three people and *Jason Junior* to a depth of 14,760 feet (4,500 m). *Jason Junior* is remotely controlled and can take video footage.

Titanic's wreck site

TIMELINE
JULY 1985 – JULY 1986

In one year, the wreck of *Titanic* was located and explored.

JULY 1985
Robert Ballard joins a team of French oceanographers on board research ship *Le Suroit*. They use a state-of-the-art sonar device, suspended from a cable 12,500 feet (3,810 m) below the ship to search for *Titanic*, but cannot locate the wreck.

AUGUST 12, 1985
Le Suroit is replaced by *Knorr*, which is equipped with *Argo*, a new and unmanned submersible vessel.

AUGUST 25, 1985
Argo is deployed from *Knorr*. The submersible's video cameras send moving TV images back to the ship showing craters on the sea bottom, possibly made by pieces of wreckage.

SEPTEMBER 1, 1985
Argo's cameras view one of *Titanic*'s boilers. *Argo* maps the debris field during the next few days, while *Knorr*'s echo sounder locates the main section of *Titanic*'s hull.

The remotely controlled vehicle *Argo*

The aft section was very badly damaged as it separated from the stern and sank.

The distance between the aft section and the bow section is about 1,970 feet (600 m).

Titanic's resting place

Titanic rests in the dark abyssopelagic zone, which extends down to 20,000 feet (6,000 m). Creatures that live here, such as anglerfish, have to put up with huge pressures.

TITANIC Tales

ROBERT BALLARD

Robert Ballard is a former officer in the U.S. Navy who became famous as an oceanographer and archaeologist. Other wrecks he has explored include the liner *Lusitania*, which was torpedoed off Ireland, and *Yorktown*, the American aircraft carrier sunk in the Battle of Midway during World War II.

Robert Ballard

The midnight zone

No light reaches the midnight zone, which extends from 3,300 feet (1,000 m) to 13,100 feet (4,000 m).

The ship left a trail of debris on the ocean floor, which led Ballard's team to the hull.

Jason Junior can explore inside the wreck of the bow section while it is still tethered to *Alvin*.

Titanic's bow section plowed into the mud on the ocean floor as it hit the bottom.

Ballard's team arrives near the wreck site on board *Atlantis II*, equipped with *Alvin* and *Jason Junior*.

JULY 14, 1986

The submersible *Alvin* comes to rest on the deck of the bow section, near the mast that held the crow's nest from which lookout Frederick Fleet saw the iceberg.

Research vessel *Knorr*

JULY 24, 1986

Ballard's team makes its final dive. Over 12 days, they have explored and photographed most of the site.

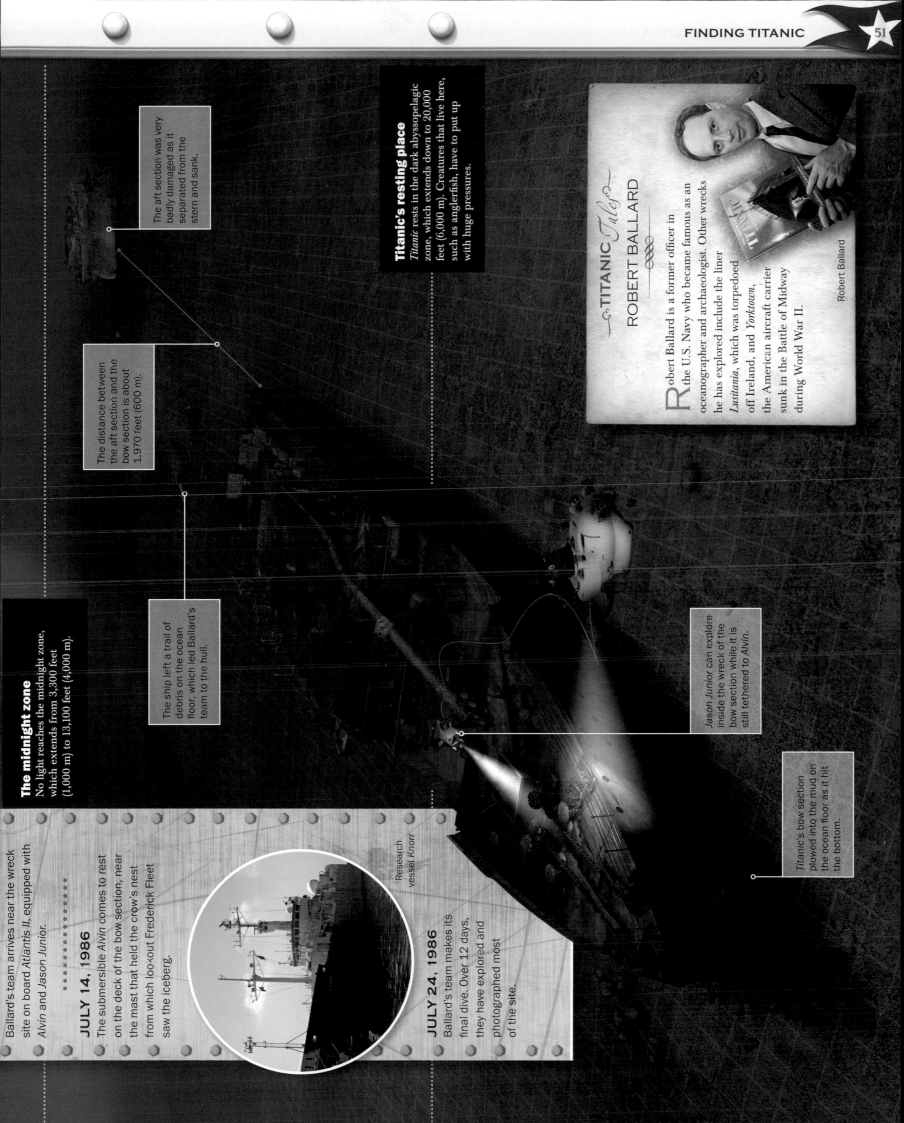

Boat deck

The decaying boat deck is covered in rusticles, which are icicle-like formations that are made by bacteria living on the wreck. They eat its rusting metal and leave behind waste products in the form of mineral compounds.

EXPLORING TITANIC

SINCE ROBERT BALLARD and his team discovered and then surveyed *Titanic*'s wreck, there have been many expeditions in submersibles to explore and photograph the ship's remains. As a result, we know more about how the vessel sank, how it broke up as it dropped to the ocean floor, and how the metal hull and fittings are gradually decaying.

In addition, explorers began to discover many artifacts—from the ship's fittings and the equipment used by the crew to the tableware from various dining rooms and the personal belongings of passengers. A company, RMS Titanic Inc., was given the right to salvage these artifacts. The company does not own the wreck or the salvaged items, and these have been cleaned and cared for, and exhibited to some 20 million visitors all over the world. As a result of this work, we know more about *Titanic* than ever before.

Wing propeller

Titanic's huge starboard propeller, which measures about 23 feet (7 m) across, was bent as it hit the seabed. Some of it is covered by rusting metal.

MIR SUBMERSIBLES

TWO SUBMERSIBLES called MIR-1 and MIR-2 are among the few vessels that can dive deeper than 9,850 feet (3,000 m). James Cameron used the MIR submersibles to film the wreck for his epic *Titanic* and for a documentary, *Ghosts of the Abyss*, that told the story of diving to the ocean bottom and exploring the remains of the ship.

MIR-2 exploring
the seabed

Unbroken tableware
Neat rows of stacked plates and dishes lie unbroken and almost undisturbed in the sand on the ocean floor.

Titanic's bow appears
in the gloom

SAVED FROM THE DEEP

DIVERS HAVE RECOVERED thousands of objects from *Titanic*. Restorers have carefully cleaned these relics so that they can be displayed in exhibitions around the world. Artifacts that have been found range from fragile banknotes and postcards to pieces of furniture and fittings attached to the vessel. Items used by the passengers—from unopened bottles of champagne to makeup jars—have helped historians find out more about the lives of the people on board.

Personal belongings
Pens, pocket watches, and items for grooming, such as brushes and razors, are among the many personal items recovered from the wreck site.

Signal telegraph from the bridge

Precious objects
The ship's pursers stuffed valuables such as jewelry into leather bags in the hope of saving them, but this bag went to the bottom of the sea.

Relics from the bridge
Salvaged items of ship's equipment include this telegraph, which was used to send messages from the bridge to the engine room.

Chipped china coffee cup

A Purser's black bag filled with jewelry

China and glassware
Divers have recovered lots of china and glass items from the wreck. This plain cup was probably used for coffee in a third-class area.

Reclining deck chair from the promenade deck

Fixtures and fittings
Metal fittings that have been salvaged include a ship's bell, a number of lamps, and this brass porthole.

Furniture
Wooden deck chairs with footrests allowed passengers to recline in comfort on deck.

A brass porthole

Silverware
These items of silver flatware, despite being corroded, show the kind of luxurious tableware used in the first-class dining room.

Silver knives and forks from the first-class dining room

A matchbox specially made for the White Star Line

WHITE STAR LINE
SAFETY MATCHES
PREPARED SPECIALLY
FOR USE ON BOARD
WHITE STAR STEAMERS
MADE IN SWEDEN

STAGE AND SCREEN

THE FIRST MOVIE about the tragedy was a short silent film called *Saved from the Titanic* (1912), starring Dorothy Gibson, who survived the disaster and wrote the script. To this day, movie-makers and audiences alike have been fascinated by the dramatic story of the ship and its sinking, as well as the extraordinary tales of survival and the glamorous lifestyle of the first-class passengers.

RECREATING THE SHIP

Several movie directors have recreated the ship by using studio sets, models and other White Star liners. The ships that can be seen in *A Night to Remember* and James Cameron's 1997 movie *Titanic* are said to be the most accurate portrayals of the liner.

Titanic (1953)

This movie tells the story of an unhappy couple and their two children. Just before *Titanic* sinks, they make up with each other, but the father and son drown.

Titanic (199_

Leonardo DiCaprio a_ Kate Winslet star in t_ gripping love story by Jam_ Cameron, which is famous _ its stunning special effec_

A Night to Remember (1958)

Kenneth More starred as Second Officer Charles Lightoller in *A Night to Remember*, which was billed as "the greatest sea drama in living memory."

SOS Titanic (1979)

The different experiences of three groups of passengers— traveling first, second, and third class—are shown in this made-for-TV movie.

Raise the Titanic (1_

A group of people raise th_ wreck of *Titanic* from the s_ bed in their search for a rar_ and valuable mineral which_ they are convinced is on bo_

Many sequences in James Cameron's *Titanic* were shot using a model that was only 46 feet (14 m) long.

MS OASIS OF THE SEAS

Oasis of the Seas sets a new record for passenger capacity and is designed to cruise the Caribbean. The ship is about twice as heavy as *Titanic*.

BUILDER: STX EUROPE, TURKU, FINLAND
OWNER: ROYAL CARIBBEAN INTERNATIONAL
LAUNCHED: NOVEMBER 22, 2008
LENGTH: 1,181 FT (360 M)   **BEAM:** 198 FT (60.5 M)
SPEED: 22.6 KNOTS (26 MPH / 41.8 KM/H)
CAPACITY: 8,461 (6,296 PASSENGERS / 2,165 CREW)

RMS QUEEN MARY 2

Although often used for cruising, *Queen Mary 2* was designed for crossing the Atlantic and has a faster speed than cruise ships, such as *Oasis of the Seas*.

BUILDER: CHANTIERS DE L'ATLANTIQUE, FRANCE
OWNER: CUNARD LINE
LAUNCHED: MARCH 21, 2003
LENGTH: 1,132 FT (345 M)   **BEAM:** 147.5 FT (45 M)
SPEED: 29.5 KNOTS (34 MPH / 54.7 KM/H)
CAPACITY: 4,309 (3,056 PASSENGERS / 1,253 CREW)

MS QUEEN ELIZABETH II

Queen Elizabeth II joined Cunard's fleet in October 2010. Decorated in the style of the 1930s and 1940s, she is the third liner to bear the name of Elizabeth.

BUILDER: FINCANTIERI MONFALCONE, ITALY
OWNER: CUNARD LINE
LAUNCHED: OCTOBER 11, 2010
LENGTH: 964 FT (293 M)   **BEAM:** 106 FT (32 M)
SPEED: 23.7 KNOTS (27.25 MPH / 43.8 KM/H)
CAPACITY: 3,064 (2,068 PASSENGERS / 996 CREW)

SUPERLINERS

TODAY, MOST PEOPLE MAKE their long-distance journeys by air, but there is still a role for large liners, such as *Oasis of the Seas*, to provide unique vacation cruises around the world's most beautiful coasts. These modern cruise liners are the descendants of *Titanic*, and they are much larger and take luxury to even higher levels.

The new Oasis-class liners, for example, pamper passengers with several swimming pools, as well as nightclubs, a casino, and courts for sports such as volleyball and basketball. Some of the onboard pools are designed to imitate beaches and there is even a park with real plants and trees. Entertainment on these superliners ranges from karaoke to computer gaming, and passenger accommodations include luxury suites with private decks or balconies.

More titanic than Titanic
The multiple decks of *Oasis of the Seas* rise 236 feet (72 m) above the waterline, roughly as high as a 24-story building, or twice the height of *Titanic*.

Fun on the high seas

A sheltered "boardwalk" with amusements (above left) and an outdoor pool with a surf simulator (above) are two of the most popular leisure facilities on *Oasis of the Seas*.

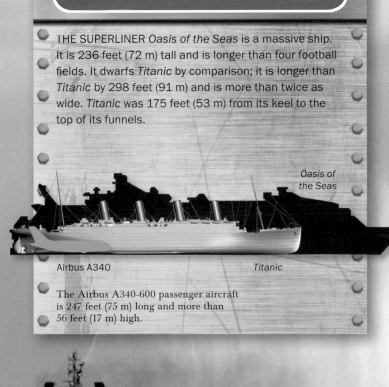

HOW BIG IS BIG?

THE SUPERLINER *Oasis of the Seas* is a massive ship. It is 236 feet (72 m) tall and is longer than four football fields. It dwarfs *Titanic* by comparison; it is longer than *Titanic* by 298 feet (91 m) and is more than twice as wide. *Titanic* was 175 feet (53 m) from its keel to the top of its funnels.

Oasis of the Seas

Airbus A340   *Titanic*

The Airbus A340-600 passenger aircraft is 247 feet (75 m) long and more than 56 feet (17 m) high.

TITANIC REMEMBERED

THE SINKING OF TITANIC affected thousands of people—the families, friends, neighbors, work colleagues, and acquaintances of all those who lost their lives. As a result, remembering and respecting the dead—their lives, talents, and the bravery with which so many faced death—has always been important. Every book and film about the ship is in part a memorial to the people who died and their experiences on the terrible night of April 14, 1912.

TRIBUTES AND MEMORIALS

Many communities have put up their own memorial statues and plaques in tribute to *Titanic*'s passengers and crew. Cities with a special connection to *Titanic*, such as Belfast where the ship was built, and Southampton from which the ship sailed, have been especially eager to make this kind of lasting tribute to those who were lost.

NAMED AT LAST

THE GRAVES OF 120 *Titanic* victims are at Halifax, Nova Scotia, Canada. One belongs to an "unknown child," whose body was not identified. In 2007 the child was named as Sidney Goodwin, aged 19 months, whose entire family perished in the disaster.

MEMORIAL LIGHT

DEDICATED EXACTLY one year after the sinking, this lighthouse memorial was originally built on top of the Seaman's Institute in New York City, and its green light was visible across the city's East River. When the Institute moved to another building, the lighthouse was relocated next to the South Street Seaport Museum.

CANADA

HALIFAX

NEW YORK

WASHINGTON, D.C.

UNITED STATES

TITANIC *Tales*

THE YOUNGEST LIVED LONGEST

Millvina Dean was the youngest survivor of *Titanic* and, until May 2009 when she died, was the last remaining and longest-lived survivor. In her later years she took part in conferences and appeared on TV and radio to talk about *Titanic*.

Millvina Dean

WOMEN HONOR BRAVE MEN

THE WOMEN OF AMERICA put up a *Titanic* memorial in Washington, D.C., in 1931. Designed by American sculptor Gertrude Vanderbilt Whitney, its granite statue has outstretched arms and commemorates the men who "gave their lives that women and children might be saved." The statue's pose was famously adopted by Kate Winslet in James Cameron's movie, *Titanic*.

LAST PORT OF CALL

QUEENSTOWN was the last place *Titanic* docked before setting out across the Atlantic. The memorial in the port (now Cobh) was installed in 1998. Its inscription remembers the many Irish people who sailed on the ship in the hope of starting new lives in the USA.

FOR THEIR DEVOTION TO DUTY

BELFAST'S MEMORIAL was erected in 1920. It was sculpted by Sir Thomas Brock and paid for partly by the White Star Line and the workers from Harland and Wolff, where *Titanic* was built. It remembers the devotion to duty of the "gallant Belfastmen" who perished with the ship.

MUSICAL HEROES

IN 1913 THE MUSICIANS' UNION paid for a memorial in Southampton to *Titanic*'s heroic musicians, who played on until the end. It was destroyed in World War II, but in 1990 a replica was unveiled. It bears the names of the band members and the words, "They died at their posts like men."

BELFAST

UNITED KINGDOM

IRELAND

COBH

SOUTHAMPTON

DUTY CALLED THEM TO THE END

MORE THAN 100,000 PEOPLE gathered in Southampton's Andrews Park to see an imposing memorial to the ship's engineers unveiled in April 1914. By staying at their posts, the engineers kept the ship's lights on, enabling others to find their way to the lifeboats.

The last image of *Titanic* afloat was taken at Queenstown.

TITANIC FACTFILE

GLOSSARY

Aft: The rear part of a ship or boat, toward or at the stern.

Beam: The width of a ship at its broadest point.

Berth: A bed or bunk in a cabin on board a ship.

Bilge: The lowest part of the hull of a ship.

Bow: The front section of a ship or boat.

Bulkhead: A partition that divides a ship into separate watertight compartments.

Cargo hold: The part of a ship's hull in which goods are carried.

Davit: A small crane used to lower lifeboats or haul cargo.

Debris field: An area of the seabed where wreckage of *Titanic* was scattered.

Echo sounder: A device used to detect objects on the seabed; it sends down sounds and measures the time their echoes take to return.

Forecastle deck: An upper deck at the bow end of a ship.

Gantry: A bridgelike framework that supports a crane or a working platform for building a ship.

Hatch: An opening in a deck leading to the hold.

Hull: The main body of a ship.

Ice field: An area of an ocean that contains icebergs.

Inquiry: A detailed investigation of an incident.

Keel: The structure running from bow to stern of a ship's hull, acting as its "backbone."

Maneuvering: Steering a ship to change its direction of travel.

Moorings: The equipment such as ropes and anchors that keeps a ship fixed in a dock.

Poop deck: The raised deck toward the stern of a ship.

Port: The left-hand side of a ship.

Premonition: A sense that something is going to happen.

Reciprocating engine: An engine with pistons that move up and down.

Lifeboat on davits

Remotely operated vehicle (ROV): A vehicle, such as a small submarine or robot, that is driven by remote control.

Rivet: A metal pin used to fix parts of a structure together.

Starboard: The right-hand side of a ship.

Stateroom: A private cabin, usually large or luxurious, on board a ship.

Steam turbine: A device that creates power when a jet of steam pushes around a bladed wheel.

Stern: The rear part of a ship or boat.

Submersible: A small vessel designed to operate underwater.

Telegraph: A system for sending messages using simple electrical signals.

Tonnage: The number of tons of water displaced by a ship when afloat.

Ventilation: A system of circulating fresh air around a vessel or building.

TITANIC ONLINE

There are many Web sites that contain information about *Titanic*. Here are four of the biggest and best of them.

http://www.Titanic.com
Group of maritime enthusiasts who have created a *Titanic* community where they can share information about *Titanic* and related subjects.

www.expeditionTitanic.com
Web site bringing together images from many different *Titanic* expeditions, creating a stunning collection of photographs of the wreck site.

www.nmni.com/Titanic
Dedicated *Titanic* site from the National Museums of Northern Ireland, full of details from original designs to moving memories.

www.encyclopedia-Titanica.org
Large site containing information about the ship, its design, construction, and voyage, plus extensive information about the crew and passengers.

Captain Smith standing next to bridge telegraph

TITANIC MISTAKES

Several mistakes in the design, building, and operation of the ship could have contributed to the sinking, or prevented more people from being rescued. Some of these have been disputed by historians.

To make more room for cabins, the bulkheads were not built high enough and water flowed from one compartment to the next, pulling the ship down.

The rivets that fixed the hull's metal plates were not made of top-quality iron.

Several warnings about ice were ignored before the ship's course was changed.

Rivets on a section of recovered hull

WHITE STAR "TITANIC"

* The steersman may have confused two kinds of orders: "Rudder orders" are used on steamships to indicate which direction to turn; the "tiller orders" used on sailing ships tell you to steer in the opposite direction.

* Titanic was said to be going too fast because Captain Smith was told to sail quickly, despite the icy conditions.

* There were too few lifeboats, and the lifeboats were not filled because there had been no practice drills on the ship.

* If nearby ships had kept their radios turned on, their crew would have known that Titanic was in trouble.

* Titanic fired only eight distress rockets.

A TITANIC MYSTERY

When *Titanic*'s radio operators were hard at work just before the collision, they were told that a mystery ship was visible near the horizon. Crew members prepared to fire rockets to send a signal to the ship, but the vessel disappeared rapidly, and no one could identify it nor explain where it had gone.

TITANIC TIME

The time of day differs from one place on the globe to another—for example, London is five hours ahead of New York. When *Titanic* was moving slowly across the sea, it was usual to adjust the time on board each day to bring it roughly in line with local time. So 12 noon on board would be the point at which the sun was at its highest point in the sky that day. This ship time is known as "Bridge Time". The time of the collision was 23:40 Bridge Time. In London the time was 03:02 and in New York it was 22:02.

INDEX

CREDITS

The publisher would like to thank Tricia Waters for the index.

ILLUSTRATIONS

Front & back cover Peter Bull Art Studio
Peter Bull Art Studio 2-3, 5bl, br, 8-9, 11tl, 16-17, 18-19, 22-23, 30-31,
34-45, 40-41, 42-43, 48-49, 56-57; Leonello Calvetti 10-13; Barry Croucher/
The Art Agency 20-21, 62br; Malcolm Godwin/Moonrunner Design 50-51;
Gary Hanna/The Art Agency 36-37, 38-39, 62tr; KJA-artists 14-15, 44-45; Iain
McKellar 42tl, cl, l, bl; Francesca D'Ottavi/Wilkinson Studios 4br, 26-27,
28-29; Roger Stewart/KJA-artists 37r, 39r, 41r, 54-55bg

PHOTOGRAPHS

Key t=top; l=left; r-right; d=top left; tr=top right; tc=top center; tcl=top center left;
tcr=top center right; c=center; cr=center right; cl=center left; b=bottom; bl=bottom
left; br=bottom right; bc=bottom center; bcr=bottom center right; bcl,bottom
center left; bg=background
ALA=Alamy; BL=British Library; CBT=Corbis; GI=Getty Images;
IS=iStockphoto.com; LC=Library of Congress; MEPL=Mary Evans Picture
Library; MQ=Maritime Quest; PIC=Picture Desk; REX=Rex Features;
TPL=photolibrary.com; Wiki=Wikipedia
Back cover bl BL, tr ALA; **6** tc ALA, br GI, cl LC, bl, c MEPL; bg MQ; **7** bc
CBT, bl, br MEPL; **8** cr CBT, c TF; **9** r MEPL, br MQ; **10** cl LC, b MQ, cr TPL;
13 r MQ, tr TPL; **14-15** MQ; **15** br LC; **16** cl TF; **17** b CBT, br IS; **18** bl MQ, tr
TF; **19** bl TF, tr MQ; **20** tr CBT; **21** tc LC; **22** bl CBT; **23** tr MQ; **24** bg IS, bl, cl
MEPL, t MQ, b CBT; **25** cr CBT, l, bcr MEPL, t, tr, bc MQ, tcr TF; **26** bl LC, tr
CBT; **27** tr LC, b, t TF; **28** l MEPL, tr LC; **29** tr TF; **30** bg IS, bl MEPL, l ALA,
tr PIC; **31** tl, cl GI, br CBT, r TF; **32** tl TPL, b MQ; **33** tr CBT; **34** tl REX; **35** IS;
36 tr GI, bl TF; **37** tr GI; **40** tr TF; **41** tl IS; **42** t LC, b MEPL; **44** t, tr MQ, cr
MEPL; **45** t ALA, bl, bc LC, c MQ; **46** bg IS, tl CBT, l LC, b TF; **47** l REX, t, tr
CBT, br PIC; **48** tr Wiki, l, b MEPL; **49** tl MEPL, tc ALA, bl, br CBT, tr Wiki;
50 bl CBT; **51** bc Wiki, tr CBT; **52-3** CBT; **54-5** CBT; **55** br MEPL; **56** tl, br
ALA, br PIC; **57** tl GI, c REX, br PIC; **58** bg CBT, tl Wiki, cl GI; **59** tl, tr CBT;
60 bl CBT, l ALA, tr IS, br TF; **61** tl, t, r ALA, tr Wiki, br MQ; endpapers GI